SOME REVIEWS OF *THE LUNAR VISITATIONS*

From a Hindu religious ceremony in Delhi to an "April Night in Harlem," Sudeep Sen's poems span cultures, ages, and myths. Evocative, poignant, and highly intelligent, *The Lunar Visitations* marks the debut of a poet of immense promise.   SHASHI THAROOR

Book deserves special note. (Sen) shows considerable talent. He catches intangible mood rather deftly. There is good poetry around.   KEKI DARUWALLA in *Sunday*

Sen (has) emotion and sensitivity ... and flash of felicitous phrase.
                                                    SHIV K KUMAR in *The Hindustan Times*

It is the poet's intense realisation of the moon as almost a persona that gives some of the best of these poems their meaning and thrust. ... As a poetic device, Sen has found an effective one. ... Sen is a poet of promise, a serious poet.
                                        ANNA SUJATHA MATHAI in *The Sunday Observer*

Feelings are wholesome, ... expressed in language that is, well, clear. His faith and unfaith have alternated to create *The Lunar Visitations*. ... A quiet questioner.
                                                    GOPAL GANDHI in *The Book Review*

An epic. Sen has patterned the poems well. ... On the ascent.
                                                    SANTAN RODRIGUES in *The Daily*

(An) unified variety makes for a thoughtful and interesting book. ... Sudeep Sen is a many-minded poet, at home equally in fantasy and social protest. And when he chooses, he can be poet of pure lyrical quality.
                            FRED CHAPPELL in *Roanoke Times & World-News* (Virginia)

The moonwashed poems in Sudeep Sen's *The Lunar Visitations* are a successful invocation to the muse, for the muse has shone on him and blessed him; these poems are his proof, our pleasure and a beginning of a long and interesting career.
                                                    WILLIAM MATTHEWS

Sudeep Sen's intimacy with a cross section of India's customs, religion and social structures makes for a poetry of compassion and understanding, in language irridescent with thought and sensitivity interacting. *The Lunar Visitations* is an important, heartfelt first book.   DAVID IGNATOW

Around the world on words ....   BEN MAPP in *The Village Voice* (New York)

The Lunar Visitations earned praise from the North Carolina Poet Laureate Sam Ragan as an excellent work. In these poems, Sen creates a strong mood which gives the poems their ultimate power and finesse.   BARBARA MAYERS in *Davidson Journal* (North Carolina)

Though sensitive to the issues of formalism and academicism in poetry, Sen's work is nevertheless structured and orderly. ... The poems are set in a triadic structure ... (He is) something of a populist concerning poetry and contemporary life.
JILL CORNFIELD in Upper West Side Resident (New York)

The poetic voice of Sudeep Sen is that of the 1980's and 90's, traversing topographical and temporal borders, and travelling with everyman on his search for truth. ... The work is striking for its evocation of the city, where Sen's words literally become the brush strokes of a painter of a such a landscape.   *L.A. India* (Los Angeles)

After Vikram Seth and his *Golden Gate*, there is a new entrant in the poetry circles. ... The moon is an important motif in (Sen's) poems, but some have a delightful human touch ....   *The Illustrated Weekly of India*

Perceptions of quiddity ... powers of observations ... clearly his plus-points.   *The Hindu*

Sen's canvas is wide and the feelings of a young man greatly affected by his milieu. Hindu and Christian thoughts mingle in his poetry. *The Lunar Visitations* is a remarkable first book of poems.   *The Statesman*

The Lunar Visitations is a sensation in Indian writing in English -- defining a new idiom.
Sunday Mail

The art of creative verse that (appeals) to one's inner ear. ... Close encounters of the lunar kind.   *The Herald*

Sen's powers of observation are his strongest points.   *Indian Review of Books*

The Lunar Visitations' lucid style and the vast colourful canvas spanning several continents transcends international barriers. Its release brings into the limelight yet another Indian writer proving mastery over the British language -- Sudeep Sen -- India's latest literary lion.   *Society*

Sen has an acute perception of the injustice and disharmony that pervade human dealings. (His) poems are richly deserving of comment. One must acknowledge the presence of a notable artist in the making.   *The India Magazine*

Critically acclaimed, a powerful first book of verse by a young poet worth watching.

Gentleman

Compactness in the use of words is the hallmark of Sen's poetry in this collection. A lot of artistry and hard work has gone into making these poems. ... Images are striking ... There is social conscience in Sen's poetry.

The Sunday Sentinel

Lucid style ... fertile imagination ... pleasing the mind.

Mid Day

The (reader) is stilled by the power of the language and landscapes coupled with the stark reality of human participation and experience. Sen's poems are crisp and clean, finely constructed and deeply felt.

Swagat

The style develops on classical verse forms, but is rarely restricted by them ... The language and structure of the poems make them accessible.

First City

(The moon's) all-pervading presence makes one almost feel as if (it) were watching quietly guiding the trends of events as the poet celebrated the *joie de vivre* through his poems.

Financial Express

A distinguished achievement. ... The book requires concentrated study. *The Evening News*

A few young Indians, especially Bengalis, have secured berths in the literary spheres of the English-speaking world. The latest addition to such a list is Sudeep Sen. ... His (poetry) is highly acclaimed ... If Michael Madhusudan Dutt were alive, he would definitely revert back to writing in English.

Ananda Bazar Patrika (Bengali)

Sudeep's poems reflects love ... world within and outside the asylum ... also depicts and paints the beauty of the moon. ... But what has attracted Jayanta Mahapatra, one of India's leading poets, is Sen's language which (Sen's) very own (with which he) is able to dramatise his keen observations with power and immediacy.

Sananda (Bengali)

Sudeep Sen's poems are robust, candid, vulnerable, by turns tender and aggressive. Tight-packed stanzas of fantasy, surreal juxtapositions, mystery and myth with rapid scene changes -- it takes time to recover from the dizzy stupor this collection puts you in. *The Lunar Visitations* gazes into life, both intense and listless, and is brilliantly conceived.

Kavya Bharati

Few people accomplish so much so early. Fewer still do it so well. Sudeep Sen belongs to that select group.

Competition & Career Times

NEW YORK TIMES

Works by Sudeep Sen

poetry

The Lunar Visitations
Kali in Ottava Rima
Durga
New York Times
(AS A FEATURED POET IN ANTHOLOGIES)
Poetry India: Emerging Voices
An Anthology of New Indian English Poetry
Poetry Now Anthology

film

Babylon is Dying: Diary of Third Street
Woman of a Thousand Fires
(WITH SUBHRA & JAYABRATO CHATTERJEE)
Kya Baat Hai
Cry Freedom
Colour My World

NEW YORK TIMES

Sudeep Sen

THE MANY PRESS
LONDON

Copyright 1993 by SUDEEP SEN

Published by
The Many Press, 15 Norcott Road, London N16 7BJ

Sudeep Sen is hereby identified as the author of this work
in accordance with Section 77 of the Copyright,
Designs and Patents Acts 1988.

Author Photo by Priti Dave

British Library Cataloguing in Publication Data
Sen, Sudeep, 1964-
New York Times
I. Title
821'.9'14

ISBN 0-907326-25-0

This is Number Twelve in The Many Press: Third Series

7|4|93

First Edition

Printed in Great Britain
by Falcon Press, Edinburgh

FOR
PHILLIS LEVIN, AARON TAYLOR,
JOY
&
PRITI

ACKNOWLEDGEMENTS

My thanks to the editors of the following publications in India, United States, and Britain, in which a number of these poems, some in earlier versions and under different titles, first appeared:

Bombay Literary Review, Book Review, Boulevard, Cargoes, Creations, Davidsonian, India Perspectives, The Illustrated Weekly of India, The Independent, Indraprastha, Indian P.E.N., Inside Art, The Journal of Poetry Society of India, Namaste: 1991 Issue on Contemporary Indian Creative Writing, Literature Alive, Of Age, Patriot, Pivot, Plum Review, Poetry, Poetry Chronicle, Poetry Now, Roots, The Roanoke Times & World-News, Window, The Telegraph, The Times of India, Swagat, Sunday Mail, Sunday Observer, The Statesman & Society.

"New York Times" which won the runners-up award in the 1991 British Council/Poetry Society of India National Poetry Competition, appears in the anthology, *Poetry India: The Emerging Voices* (New Delhi: Clarion Books, 1992)

Few of the poems also appear in the anthology *New Indian English Poetry* (New Delhi: Rupa & Co, 1993) and *Poetry Now Anthology* (Petersborough, UK: Poetry Now, 1993)

"Scattered Pieces of a Quarrel" which won the third prize in the 1990 All India Poetry Circle Competition, appears in the society's journal, *Poesis*.

"Harlem" (in an earlier version) first appeared in *The Lunar Visitations* (New Delhi: Rupa & Co., 1991, and New York: White Swan Books, 1990).

The prose piece "Treading the Season's First Snow" first appeared in *Network.*

Many of these poems have been broadcast on *All India Radio*, New Delhi, *Radio Tehran*, Tehran, *RTM 103.8 FM*, London, *WFUV 90.7 FM Radio*, New York, and *Channel 56 Television*, Washington, D.C.

Extracts of some of the poems have also been used in the following films: *Woman of a Thousand Fires, Cry Freedom*, and *Colour My World.*

Acknowledgements are also due to an unknown benefactor and to the GBM Trust with whose technical assistance the production of this book was made possible.

I wish to thank the Inlaks Foundation in London for their grant in 1988-89, during which time a few of these poems were first written.

I am grateful to The Arvon Foundation in Devon for the Faber & Faber poetry grant which allowed me to participate in a week-long workshop residency with some wonderful poets.

Various people have been extremely cooperative and helpful in many different ways during my poetic assignments in Britain. The list is too long to name each one of them, my thanks to everyone. However, I would especially like to express my gratitude to Ranjana Ash, Alastair Niven and Peter Forbes for their insight and advice on numerous matters.

Special thanks to Phillis Levin who saw these poems through their infancy and providing criticism, to Anthony Abbott and Joy for mid-wifing them and sharing their comments, to John Welch for taking this project on with grace in spite of acute time commitments, and most of all, to Priti who provided strength and calm.

Finally, I would like to thank Tessa Ransford and The Scottish Poetry Library in Edinburgh for their support and unhindered space, where during the first phase as their poet-in-residence this winter, I worked on the final draft of this book.

CONTENTS   **PAGE**

To Europe she was America, to America
she was the gateway of the earth.
But to tell the story of New York
would be to write a social history of the world.
        H. G. WELLS, *The War in the Air*, Ch. 6

New York's a small place
when it comes to the part of it that wakes up
just as the rest is going to bed.
        P. G. WODEHOUSE,
        The Aunt and the Sluggard, *My Man Jeeves*

I think that New York is not the cultural centre
of America, but the business and administrative
centre of American culture.
        SAUL BELLOW, *Listener*
        May 22, 1969 (radio interview)

A sallow waiter brings me beans and pork . . .
Outside there is fury in the firmament.
Ice-cream, of course, will follow; and I'm content.
O Babylon! O Carthage! O New York!
        SIEGFRIED SASSOON, *Storm on Fifth Avenue*

I

MANHATTAN

They are men on the run,
Fuelled by bourbon and fear
Of things slipping away from them.

ALAN ROSS, Wall Street
Death Valley & Other Poems in America

NEW YORK TIMES

Every morning in relentless hurry, I scurry
through the streets of New York, turn around the avenue, flee
            past the red and white awning of the Jewish deli,
        walk out with a bagel or croissant or spilled coffee,
        disappearing underground in a flurry,

speeding in a subway of mute faces, barely swallowed the bite,
barely unfolded *The Times*, barely awake.
            Before I realise, it's lunch-time, and then,
        soon it is evening, late,
        being herded home with the flow of humankind,

up and down elevators, escalators, staircases, and ramps. I am
back on the streets again, late night,
            though early enough to glance at the headlines
        of next morning's paper. In this city, I
        count the passage of time only by weekends

linked by five-day flashes I don't
even remember. In this city where walking means
            running, driving means speeding, there seem to exist
        many days in one, an ironical and oblique
        efficiency. But somewhere, somehow, time takes its toll,

malnourished, overburdened, and overutilised,
as the tunnels seeping under the river's belly slowly cave
            in, the girders lose their tension like old dentures, and
        the underground rattles with the passing of every train.
        After all, how long can one stretch time?

Illusions can lengthen, credit ratings strengthen,
even Manhattan elongates with every land-fill,
            but not time, it takes its own time, still,
      the way it always has and always will,
      not a second more, not a second less.

RAIN ON HOT CONCRETE

After the sweltering heat of the day,
    the evening fumed in its aftermath

while the lissome jogger's rhythmic sway
    on the sidewalk, cantered, as

the rubber of the sole sprung
    at every contact with the tarmac,

while the laden sky donned
    a coat of grey, furthering that

weight, adding to the unusual calm. Somehow the
    runner's five-mile stretch seemed longer

today, as a sheet of sweat glued her
    cotton tights to her

body: taut, tenuous, every curve and muscle,
    sculpted. Her skin glistened with

exhaustion and the spray of intermittent drizzle,
    as the moisture of the sky and the skin

met the cement of the concrete in a sizzle,
    smouldering, smelling of stale steam.

SCATTERED PIECES OF A QUARREL

We listen while a dustpan eats
the scattered pieces of a quarrel.
VERN RUTSALA

Every night, for many years now I hear voices next door
through the thin of the wall, every core

of the crackling scream, like an old
stylus needle on a scratched gramophone record,

stuck. Every night it happens, shriller and fiercer
every night. At midnight, the ritual starts over:

the first conversations barely audible,
then the decibel levels, a plateau of maimed muffles

before taking off sharply, into the crystal
air of coded cries, on a steep delirious climb until

breaking glass-ware scatter smithereens
as the soprano of anguish startles a bluebird in

the nest outside, on the terracotta ledge
of my alcove. Every morning when the sun's edge

clears the neighbour's roof, I sweep the apartment floor
trying to extricate rolls of dust from under the doors.

They somehow seem to huddle in fluffy balls
insulating the crevices between adjacent flats, the same wall

that simultaneously separates and shares, just like the array
of dust coils clinging together, in fear of being swept away.

SUN STREAKS ON TELEPHONE LINES

In Japanese she said it was *amae,*
though the translation provided only a weak

dependency. The telephone rang all night, the next day,
and on and on for a whole year, in

metaphoric exchanges as the pulse
matched the tones. Tones of a new language

defied the stasis of the existing ones.
Even the sun's power couldn't scorch the linkage,

its rays streaking into a Brooklyn apartment, to cast
its bleach, roasting the innards, and a human being.

The same sun in the evening spread over the vast
view: over blackened roof-tops and the rippled bay,

its light tinting the metallic verdure of the Statue
of Liberty, the geometric axes of lower Manhattan towers,

and the silver criss-cross of telephone lines. On cue,
the calls came through, regardless, from another

island, the lines humming, *"amae, amae, amae."*
Amae it had to be, after all, telephones work only on the

dependency of their senders and receivers, or else
why would such lines exist. The

sun had set long over the East River peninsula,
but had left enough energy stored, in excess,

for the unfinished conversation to carry on, with her,
undeterred, in glinting solar pulses.

HARLEM

A boy sauntered around the city
tripping, smoking pot.
Holes, cracked asphalt,

termite-eaten doors
opened right onto the sidewalks.
Behind the wooden closures

lives were made, and a crippled
man, supported on wooden stilts,
begged on one leg.

The boy, one among others,
like insects clustering
around a half-devoured carcass.

Only difference here:
the boy, the cripple,
the man, and the whore

were pecking at the same
flesh, hung on sale
on bombed-out ghetto racks.

NIGHT IN TIMES SQUARE

At two in the morning at Times Square, I
    see steam escaping from man-hole crevices
as its fumes screen the changing colours
    of the competing neon signs.
A homeless totters across the street,
    stiff and cold, totally unstartled
by the frantic yellow cab that misses
    hitting him by a mere inch.
Late nighters like me, amblers, whores,
    all gesture in silence,
in a language unknown, understanding
    each other with an everyday skill,
as the chorus of horns drown their murmur
    scintillating with the tiniest flicker of
the many-coloured cathode tubes
    illuminating the peculiar normal night.
A tiny island country
    capsules a continent, innocuously, just
as the typical night envelops the square.
    I started walking southward,
down one of the avenues, hear
    the subway underground, its rattles
fleeing the iron-grates on the streets.
    Through the silhouette of the buildings,
appears a patch of night sky, and part of
    the moon, pale orange, reflected faintly,
in the glass and steel canyon
    of downtown, in the city of dreams.

SEXLESS LIKE ALPHABETS

We are all sexless, like a line of
alphabet letters in a classroom.
ANONYMOUS

From the first babbles of a newborn lisping
to the ashed annihilation of the last skeleton,

mnemonically, life proceeds, pulsing
letter by letter, word by word, passing the baton

beat after beat, through stuttered phrases to polished facility
of language, and finally to that silence of inevitability.

That incipient whiff in the powdered spring air
of sprinkled pollen seeds and sprung stamens, prepare

to be stung, sucked, siphoned, and sipped
by the venerable black bee that carried -- the lessons of love --

spelled out, slowly, one after another, pencilled
and documented between leaves, lettered in clotted mauve.

That a man here and a woman there, mistakes
the one for the other, stand listless, admiring, regardless of sex.

That all of us, huddled together in chronological acts --
classrooms of meaning, learned and unlearned facts,

facts that fiction fulfilled and knowledge informed, existing like alphabets, like flowers, like men and women.

We, distinguishable, unseparate, pure as womb, sexless, living entities indivisible, unhindered, passionate, whole, and human.

II

SEVEN SONNETS

INSIDE CLOSED EYES, EVEN THE STONES COME ALIVE

> *held motionless by the dead*
> JON SILKIN, *Six Cemetary Poems, I*

> *Inside closed eyes,*
> *close the eyes again,*
> *even the stones come alive.*
> WIM WENDER, *Wings of Desire*

This grey tombstone bears a name, letters looping in seriffed tails,
a monogram, some dates, and something in parentheses, effaced.

    The sun rises very early in this part of the country, cross-
    lighting only the solitary visitor who braves the frost.

Every morning for years, a woman in black stole, solemn, pale,
lights three candles and places a red flower on the tombstone crest

    that sits squarely, cracked, moss-ridden, wedged by two rocks
    amidst overgrown weeds, discarded wreaths, and a shrub of

thyme. With eyes closed, hands clasped, and body wrapped in dark linen,
kneeling, she prays long, silently, alone, with no one else alive, except

    for the monolithic crowd of stone slabs and epitaphs.
    She whispers to the stone at the close of every ritual, and

the inscriptions on the rugged granite listen, while
the stone shifts at the end of her prayer, staring wide-eyed.

PENUMBRA

The sun quite unexpectedly came back out
      from behind the deep-folded rain clouds

after many days of ruffled uncertain
light. It emerged robed in tethered linen,

just the way I held the sky in my hand
like a piece of crumpled paper. Bands

      of deep blue didn't seem to interfere with
            the whites, and the cotton patches, which

were so transient, moved at the slightest
hint of breeze. I released the paper from my fist,

tried to iron out the creases and to rearrange,
but couldn't. The folds had created a new terrain

      just as the clouds in the sky never
            repeat the same pattern over, ever.

THE LEAFED CYNOSURE

The July sun shone full flame, parching the soil
in the curved ceramic pot, the same gritty reddish-brown soil

that once firmly rooted and cradled the deep green
plant in the centre of the room, now lean,

wearily arching, aching, entwined in thirst,
remembering its early days, how during the first

few months in this house, a woman tenuously cared
for each leaf, each twist of a twig, watching how it fared.

Now it hangs, like old clothes in an untouched closet, season
after season, suspended side by side, creased for no reason.

The chlorophyll, almost gone now, bleached
with every sting of the old moths, who have reached

the hollow of every strand, every fibre of the fabric's weave,
as the stem stands, white, lifeless as a fossil frieze.

SILK STRANDS FROM MY COFFIN

The silk threads you carelessly (or perhaps purposely) left behind
    are memoir-shreds whose tangled currents float
in through the unsuspecting cracks of my mind,
    awakening the scent that finally slew my throat.

Even masked, occasionally, when that air leaks in, I don't know
    whether to weave a shroud of dead silkworms, or whether
to preserve them as one forgotten frozen garland. But I do know
    that the perfume of those wilted petals will quietly linger,

just as fresh as all those once incipient light-green buds
    in our brownstone apartment's window-garden, which flocked
furiously, crowding, showering pollen every Spring. Colour-flood
    that spilled everywhere when we'd first met, now remains locked

in my coffin. I carry remembrances only of the good times before,
even though I cannot and shall never touch you again, anymore.

TRIPLE SONNET FOR THE MINIMALIST, or
A MODERN SONNET SEQUENCE for
THE SELF-ABSORBED 20TH-CENTURY BEE

1. Prodigy: Breaking-In

A bee
    came buzzing in
through
    the break in the wire
mesh
    guarding the window
space
    in the kitchen, nosing
for
    another hive that was
not
    there, humming for his
queen
    who had left his home.

2. Over-Achiever

Counter
>in the
kitchen,
>spectred with
crumbs,
>left after a
rushed
>breakfast --
spilled
>honey, bread,
butter --
>left
open,
>untended.

3. Burnt-Out: Suicide

Black
        looping antennae,
three
        not two,
probed
        into a jar that
contained
        a familiar scent,
pierced,
        and sank -- a viscous
descent,
        trapped, absorbed
in
        his own sweet sap.

III

GREENWICH VILLAGE

"Each ray of sunshine is seven minutes old,"
Serge told me in New York one December night.

"So when I look at the sky, I see the past?"
"Yes, Yes," he said. "especially on a clear day."

AGHA SHAHID ALI, Snow on the Desert
A Nostalgist's Map of America

TREADING THE SEASON'S FIRST SNOW

Everything outside my apartment bay-window right now looks so beautiful -- the soft snow flakes slowly covering the wrought-iron gates, the brownstone stoops, the scattered garbage bags, and even the shrouded people. A white crystalline sheath glimmering in an unannounced irregularity clothed all, scantily white-washing objects that otherwise went unnoticed to an everyday eye. It was the season's first snow, barely a few hours old, here in New York City.

I first noticed this altered spectacle outside, when I went to the kitchen to make my ritual late evening cup of Nestle's lemon iced-tea. I wouldn't have really known that it was snowing had not the perennial rumble of the trusty old refrigerator in my apartment miraculously ceased for a moment. In this rare absence of the cold storage hum, I heard the wispy shapes of these flickering prisms pirouette outside, as they perched on the tarmac, wavering somewhat, in the light wind.

Though, I must admit that this is a rarity, that such a sound, and that too at such a low poetic decibel could be heard, in the city where the predominant signature tunes are that of the sirens of police cars, ambulances and fire-engines.

The first snow of every season brings out in me, my instinctive habit of rediscovering neighbourhoods where I reside, to walk around and soak the sharpness in the air, leaving footprints on the transient white veil.

So unfailingly, I got out of my apartment on 84 Charles Street that stands in an area triangulated by Bleecker Street and Seventh Avenue South. It is an old, well-maintained pre-war building, a brownstone of sorts, with only five floors. In an age where tall glass and steel frameworks dominate the cityscape, Greenwich Village still maintains its quaint characteristics. Many of the streets here are amiably bordered with trees, dotted with varied shops selling anything from Burmese beer and Chinese black-bean sauce, to unusual art nouveau stores, gay bars, and galleries.

You have probably heard of Washington Square Park where you can find New York University students, frisbee aficionados, volleyball players, musicians, modern day Bohemians, and the people who like to watch them all. You have perhaps also heard of Sheridan Square and Christopher Street with its host of cafes, bars and night clubs. But perhaps you might not have visualised Grove Court, the lovely and secluded row of 19th Century houses near the corner of Grove and Bedford Streets (where O. Henry lived), or the pier at Morton Street on River Hudson from which on a crisp day you can see the familiar Statue of Liberty.

But the Village is so much more than just that. The community activists are struggling hard to keep control of their famous and much-loved neighbourhood. You can still find the meat-packing factories of the 1920s, old speakeasies, now turned into restaurants, immaculate brownstones on quiet tree-lined streets like mine, and even a Times Square miniature on West 8th Street.

If there is anywhere in Manhattan you need a map, it's right here in Greenwich Village. Nowhere else on this island would you be able to find, for example, West 4th Street bisecting West 12th Street. And such an event is not unusual or even an exception here. For a person who thinks of Manhattan as being a smooth perfectly symmetrical grid, he might be quite baffled here. It is somewhat like old parts of other cities where neighbourhoods and street patterns naturally grew with time and changed with history, and history this area certainly has. In spite of that if you get lost while ambling, the villagers are very helpful and will try to answer your queries, besides it is also a nice way of getting to know them.

Washington Square, apart from being a vibrant quadrangle of space and activity, is also marked for The Arch -- New York's answer to Paris' Arc de Triomphe. The northern-end, houses some beautiful homes, including #7 where Edith Wharton lived.

Strolling down Bleecker Street, I passed cafes which were bustling inside in spite of the outdoor sections being closed. The awnings and the fixed furniture on the sidewalks which serve as extensions to the cafes were all snow covered. I also passed head shops, falafel parlours, jazz clubs like the *Village Gate*, paid homage to Eugene O'Neill at the *Provincetown*, and stopped for a steaming cup of cappuccino at *Caffe Dante*. If you are in the area, you should wander down some of the side streets, like Thompson, MacDougal (Bob Dylan's old stomping ground), and Sullivan.

I decided to go toward Fifth Avenue. This is where the more affluent Villagers reside. The Salmagundi Club built in 1853 near 12th Street is the last of the imposing private mansions that once lined the avenue. I passed one of my *alma maters*, The New School for Social Research, which looked rather shut at this point of the night. I did a diploma in 16mm film production there a few summers ago when I made a short feature titled, *Woman of a Thousand Fires*. The school offers a wide latitude of courses, everything from fixing a faucet leak to ethnomusicology.

Jefferson Market Library on the Avenue of Americas (6th Avenue & 10th Street) is one of the most unusual buildings in the village. Built in 1858 it is Italian Gothic in style, and served as a courthouse for many years. Across the street is *Balducci's* with its incredible selection of exotic foods, including meats, seafood, poultry, cheeses, breads, pastries, fresh fruit, and vegetables. *Famous Ray's Pizza* -- the place in the corner with long lines even on a chilly day -- is considered one of the sources for some of the best pizza in the city. I'll vouch for every slice, my favourite being the hard crusted ones with meatballs and spinach, topped with extra cheese.

Further west are a series of small winding streets with some especially interesting places to explore. $75^{1}/_{2}$ Bedford Street is the house in which Edna St. Vincent Millay and John Barrymore once lived (not at the same time). It is only nine feet wide. *Chumley's* on the same street which used to be a speakeasy during Prohibition, now has good food and poetry readings inside. I come here very often and remember having enjoyed reading from my own work once.

There is so much in this area that every time I take a walk I discover some interesting new facet of this neighbourhood. For instance -- Morton Street is often mistaken for Hester Street, because it was the site of filming *Hester Street*, a 1975 film about the Lower East Side Jewish immigrants -- Number 6 Leroy Street, built in 1880 was the home of the New York Mayor Jimmy Walker -- *White Horse Tavern* on Hudson Street was Bob Dylan's hangout on his trips to New York.

Through this tavern's frosty glass, I spotted a familiar face. So I went in to say hello, and to toast Dylan Thomas' verse, Bob Dylan's lyrics, my friend Barbara's beautiful face, and the season's first snow.

Greenwich Village, New York City

IV

REMEMBERING NEW YORK CITY FROM ELSEWHERE

. . . even a centenarian
would blow in the wind
of flowers, on
the hills of New York.

DONALD HALL, Southwest of Buffalo
The One Day & Poems 1947-1990

THIRD WEEK OF AUGUST

1

From Bread Loaf Inn's wooden porch, leaning
over the painted bannisters, I looked out: over

the low stone wall with an open gate, idling,
over a million blades of grass, grazing, over

scattered clusters of tiny yellow flowers
that powdered the fall air with whiffs of pollen.

It was the season's end, and soon however,
within a week without any warning

the grass was cut, rolled, and tied; and they sat
flat, squatting squarely on the rolling turf.

Wheat-coloured bales freckled the landscape as
the bleached grass ended in seasoned sun

spots. Farther, across the meadow in the woods,
I could hear the stream gurgling over

pebbles, a cricket's shrill whistle, an old bull
frog's croak, and the small sparrow's endless twitter.

That afternoon as I lay on the mown grass reading
my mother's letter, the sunlight filtered through

each word, each phrase, each fibre, separating
from the page, the ink's deep-blue hue.

But beyond all the obvious senses,
someone else like me who also watched, wrote, and read,

saw in a flicker of flash, two distinct images:
surf, and sun's scorching rays scarring a blade's edge.

     2

A year later in New York, the same summer dawned.
Now, each moment finely refracted, set in a violet

mosaic. For one, it appeared as a dream, a dream of
light, of life, of words, of rhythm. And softly set

in an untold metre for the other, it was a long
song, sung in inseparable couplets.

Vermont & New York

SULPHUR

1

At dawn on Riverside Drive, after the frost
clears the trees, bare twigs usually glisten

at their ends, and remnant water globules
soon disappear at the call of the sun.

But this morning, after the hoar unwrapped the bark,
I saw new blooms, tiny, delicate, arched:

green sulphur on match-heads
glowing at the very first hint of light.

2

At the same time, many longitudes east,
across ranges, deserts, and canyons,

a forest fire raged at Yellowstone.
Some spent sulphur erupted at first strike

as all the trees in an unified forest
burned in a choral conflagration.

Next morning, when the mist cleared,
every piece of bark, every branch, every twig

stood petrified, charred in columns of ash.
There were no globules glowing at the ends

as all the moisture was completely soaked
by the parched platoons of dead cinder.

There was no way to control the fire
just as there is no way to control the rain.

People, even experts, said the cycle
had to continue to its end.

Ashes, they say, replenish the earth,
soil for a new birth. In the distance,

the pyre's sacred sulphurous spirals
looped, linking the earth and the sky.

New York & Yellowstone National Park

THE LAST FLIGHT

I dreamt -- I saw an eagle -- I flew as high
as he did -- but that was the night before.

* * *

Engines roared: within seconds, screeching up the runway,
the plane soared, cutting through the San Francisco fog,
arcing over the Golden Gate that hung cabled
and suspended, stretching over the rippled bay.

Soon a thick blanket separated the city and the sky.
Through the clouds patched in parts, we viewed
what was below: black, with blinking office lights and neon,
like stars of an unusual night.

* * *

The engine's hum became a familiar groan, no longer grating
after thousands of miles at thirty-five thousand feet.

Trolleys rolled in, cans popped, ice cubes clinked,
and the liquid in the glass refracted the plaster

smile of the stewardess, draped and sterile.
We flew all night. Next morning, as sun streaked

its sharp rays through pressure-partitioned plexiglass,
I woke up, looked out: spotted roof tops,

square stretches of rust-brown land framed
by long lines of pipelines and trimmed tarmac.

Nothing outside was close by except the tips of the wings
and a lone grey eagle that had come too close.

The plane shuddered, and moments later
the captain announced there was turbulence in the air.

Fastened to the seats, I felt the plane tilt toward the left
and saw part of the eagle's wing under the metal span.

We landed soon after, probably in New York,
though much earlier than we were supposed to.

* * *

This morning I glanced at the newspaper headlines:
    flight makes an emergency landing,
left engine damaged severely by a bird-hit.

I stumbled into the kitchen to make myself some coffee,
    a few frayed feathers and a broken beak lay charred
on the stove. But then, I could have just been imagining,

half asleep at that time of the day.
    But I did know one thing: I had seen an eagle,
first in my dream, then yesterday, and again this morning.

San Francisco & New York

Born in New Delhi, India, in 1964, Sudeep Sen read at St. Columba's School and received his BA (HONOURS) from the University of Delhi. He was an International Scholar at Davidson College, received an MA from Hollins College, and as an Inlaks Scholar he completed an MS from the Graduate School of Journalism at Columbia University in New York.

His first documentary film *Babylon is Dying* was nominated for the American Academy of Television Arts & Sciences Student Emmy Award. Since then, he has made four more films, including a seven-part television serial.

Sen's first collection of poems *The Lunar Visitations* (published in the United States by White Swan Books and in India by Rupa & Co.) received a Bread Loaf Writers Conference Working Scholarship and the Vereen Bell Runner-Up Award. In 1990 he won the Third Prize in the All-India Poetry Circle Competition, and last year, the Runners-Up Award in the British Council/Poetry Society of India National Poetry Competition. Most recently, he was awarded the Faber & Faber poetry grant from the Arvon Foundation in England.

His writings have widely appeared in India, America, and Great Britain in leading newspapers and magazines such as *Boulevard, Poetry, Times of India, Illustrated Weekly of India, Times Literary Supplement, Poetry Review, London Magazine, The Telegraph, The Independent, The Statesman & Society,* amongst others.

Sudeep Sen has been recently commissioned to guest edit a portfolio of Contemporary Indian Poetry for *The Paris Review.*

A broadsheet *Durga* (Edinburgh: PDS) and a pamphlet of his poems *Kali in Ottava Rima* (London: Paramount) appeared last year. *New York Times* is Sen's first appearance in book-form in England.

Currently, he is the poet-in-residence at The Scottish Poetry Library in Edinburgh where he is simultaneously working on his next two collections, *Blue Nude* and *Songs Sung in Inseparable Couplets.*

SOME BOOKS IN THE MANY PRESS SERIES

Quiet Facts by ANTHONY BARNETT
Were There by ANDREW CROZIER
Three Poems by TIM DOOLEY
The Book, The Bay, The Breakfast by JEREMY HARDING
Winter is Not Gone by ANTHONY HOWELL
The Metro Poems by PETER HUGHES
Listening to the Stones by NICHOLAS JOHNSON
The Boy Under the Water by MARTHA KAPOS
Two Poems by JUDITH KAZANTSIS
Near Cavalry NICHOLAS LAFITTE
Bar Magenta by SIMON MARSH & PETER HUGHES
Glow-Worms by ROD MENGHAM
Signs by PETER MIDDLETON
Overdrawn Account by PETER ROBINSON
New York Times by SUDEEP SEN
The Gifted Child by W G SHEPHERD
Time Over Tyne by COLIN SIMMS
The Country of Rumour by JAMES SUTHERLAND-SMITH
Nods by GIORGIO VERECCHIA
The Eye of the Storm by IRVING WEINMANN
Erasures by JOHN WELCH
The Plains of Sight by NIGEL WHEALE

———

THE MANY PRESS has been publishing books,
pamphlets, and broadsheets of poetry since 1975.
For further details of previous publications
and a complete annotated checklist,
please write to the Press.